Life is Like a Mountain

Lessons for the Climber

Illustrated for Women

James S. Harper
Author of: Life is Like a River

Copyright © 2025 James S. Harper
All images were generated by Open AI, Chat GPT,
and edited by James S. Harper including the cover art.
All rights reserved. No part of this book may be reproduced or used in any
manner without the written permission of the author.

Hardcover Color ISBN: 979-8-9924834-4-4

First Edition

Visit the book's companion web site at WhatAboutLife65.wordpress.com.
James S. Harper earned his degree in Psychology from Kent State University.

Life is Like a Mountain

Lessons for the Climber

You asked me what I think about life.

That's not a small question, you know.
It's been lingering in the back of my mind for a while,
never with a clean answer.

But just the other night, we were sitting out back,
Remember?

The sky had gone soft,
that last bit of gold slipping through the trees.
Sort of like it is now…
though tonight, it's even more brilliant.

And something about that moment
brought a quiet kind of clarity . . .
to this thought that's been brewing.

Yeah.
I've got something to share.

Now, it might sound a little odd at first,
But hang with me.

To me, life sometimes feels like a mountain.

Not the kind you admire from a distance,
painted purple in the evening sky.

I mean the kind you climb.

Step after step.
Breath after breath.
Until you discover
what awaits at the top.

At the base,
we all start the same.

Full of energy.
Full of dreams.

The peak is hidden in the clouds.
We can't see the way,
but we feel it calling.

Some trails are wide and easy,
cleared long ago.
Others are narrow, rocky,
barely more than a hint of path.

And some?
They vanish into the woods,
leaving you to wonder
if you're even headed the right way.

At first, the trail is kind.
The ground is soft.
The trees are tall and welcoming.

You laugh easily,
make friends along the path.

Some stay with you,
matching your stride.

Some walk ahead,
faster, eager to reach the top.

And some linger behind,
their pace slower,
their story different.

You wave goodbye,
but soon,
their path fades behind.

That's how it goes.
Every step forward
is also a step apart.

And in those early miles,
there is wonder everywhere.

The scent of pine.
The song of a hidden stream.
The way the light bends through leaves.

You feel strong,
hopeful,
like the whole mountain is cheering you on.

Life feels easy.

You think—
I was made for this.

But soon,
the ground steepens.

The sun fades.
The air grows thinner.

Your feet ache.
Your breath grows short.
Your backpack feels heavy.

And the questions begin.
Am I strong enough?
Is this worth it?
Do I belong here?

The mountain is listening,
but it does not answer.

A storm rolls in.

Cold rain stings your face.
Wind lashes across the cliffs.

Your clothes cling to your skin.
Your boots slip on the rocks.

You can't see the trail.
You can't see the peak.
You can barely see what's in front of you.

And in that moment,
you wonder—
Do I turn back?

Some do.
And that's okay.

But if you stay,
if you take one more step,
and then another,
you discover something hidden deep inside.

Strength.

Patience.

A will you didn't know you had.

The storm is still fierce.
The rocks are still sharp.

But somehow—
you are still moving.

And that is enough.

Sometimes the trail lifts
to a high ridge.

You climb and climb,
your heart pounding,
your legs burning.

And then—
you reach the crest.

This must be it.
I've made it.

You celebrate.
You breathe.

But when you look up,
you see another peak waiting.

Higher.
Harder.
Still ahead.

It can break your heart.
But it also whispers:
Keep going.

That's the thing about mountains.
They don't just show you the view.
They change you on the way up.

Your legs grow stronger with every step.
Your lungs expand with every breath.
Your heart learns patience with every beat.

Step by step,
you become the kind of person
who can climb.

You don't notice it at first.
But one day,
you pause,
look back at how far you've come,
and realize—
you are not the same.

Sometimes,
you walk alone.

Sometimes,
you meet someone new,
their path weaving into yours.

You share stories.
You share silence.
You share strength.

For a while,
the climb feels lighter.

But not everyone walks the same mountain forever.
Some drift away.
Some stop to rest.
Some choose another path altogether.

It hurts to let go.
But the mountain keeps leading you upward.

There are miles
that feel endless.

Switchback after switchback.
The same rock,
the same pine tree,
the same sky,
again and again.

You wonder if you've made a mistake.
If the summit even exists.

But the only way to find out
is to keep climbing.

One step.
Then another.
Then another.

The trees fall away.
The air grows sharp and thin.

The world opens wide below you—
valleys, rivers, forests,
all stretched out like a map.

It feels like you can see forever.
And for the first time,
you believe—
Maybe I will make it.

And then, one day—
you crest the summit.

The view is wide.
Breathtaking.

You see farther than you ever thought possible.
You feel a silence that speaks louder than words.
And for a moment, the struggle makes sense.

Life unfolds in quiet clarity.

The world feels whole.

You stay there for a while.
Some stay longer—
soaking in every ridge and valley.
Others see new mountains
shining in the distance
and know they'll climb soon.

Some feel their journey is complete—
this was their summit,
their story to teach.

But here's what surprises most people:
No one rules the summit forever.
It can be home for a season,
a role,
a calling,
a dream fulfilled.

But sooner or later,
the climb begins again.
The summit isn't the end.
It's just a moment.

A moment that shows you who you are,
and what you're capable of.

When it's time, you move on.

At first,
it feels strange.
After all that effort—
to be going the other way.

But soon you realize,
you're not losing anything.
You're bringing something with you.

The strength in your legs.
The courage in your heart.
The steadiness in your stride.

These stay with you.
No one can take them away.

You carry it into the valley.
Into the days that feel ordinary.

Into the moments when no one is watching.
Into the quiet work of living.

One mountain is behind you,
but the lessons are inside you.

And they make you ready
for whatever comes next.

And sometimes,
you walk beside someone else.

You steady them when they slip.
They steady you when you stumble.

You share the climb.
You share the view.
You share the strength you earned.

The mountain taught you—
so now you can teach, too.

And here's the thing about mountains—
once you've climbed one,
the world never looks the same.
Horizons stretch wider.
Paths you couldn't see before
now lie in plain view.

And that view pulls you
toward the next mountain.

Sometimes, you're already planning it
before you've even finished the descent.

Other times, you rest in the valley,
smiling at new climbers
just beginning their journey.

You remember what it felt like
to stand where they stand—
the weight of the pack,
the hope in their eyes.

And you feel fondness.
Gratitude.
Because you know what the climb can give.

And then—
there are other mountains.

No two the same.

Each one waiting.
Each one calling.

Some you'll climb.
Some you'll admire from afar.
Some you'll leave for others.

And that's okay.

Some mountains you climb young.
Fast, reckless, laughing.

Others you climb older.
Slower, wiser,
knowing the cost.

Some you climb alone.
Some with companions.

Some carrying little.
Some carrying much.

But all of them shape you.
Every single one.

There will be days
you stop,
look back,
and see the trail winding below.

The storms you survived.
The cliffs you scaled.
The ridges you crossed.

You'll wonder how you ever made it.
And then you'll smile,
because you did.

That's the gift of the mountain.

Not just the peaks.
Not just the views.
But the climb itself.

Every step shapes you.
Every storm forges you.
Every summit teaches you.

And those lessons?
They're yours forever.

So don't worry too much
about how high the mountain is.
Or how long it takes.
Or whether you'll reach the top before the clouds roll in.

Just climb.

Because the mountain will meet you
with every step you take.

There will always be another mountain.
Another climb.
Another chance to rise.
And if you keep going—
if you keep climbing—
one day,
you'll look up from the trail,
feel the air on your face,
see the sky open wide,
and know—

This is life.

Keep climbing.

www.ingramcontent.com/pod-product-compliance
Lightning Source LLC
Chambersburg PA
CBRC091935130526
44582CB00050B/189